David Eckstein

and the ST. LOUIS CARDINALS

2006 WORLD SERIES

by Michael Sandler

Consultant: Jim Sherman
Head Baseball Coach
University of Delaware

BEARPORT
PUBLISHING

New York, New York

Credits

Cover and Title Page, © Dilip Vishwanat/Getty Images; 4, © REUTERS/Rebecca Cook; 5, © Brad Mangin/MLB Photos via Getty Images; 6, © R.D. Moore/Courtesy University of Florida Gators Sports Information Department; 7, © Courtesy University of Florida Gators Sports Information Department; 8, © REUTERS/Jeff Mitchell; 9, © John Grieshop/MLB Photos via Getty Images; 10, © Diamond Images/Getty Images; 11, © Focus On Sport/Getty Images; 12, © John Grieshop/MLB Photos via Getty Images; 13, © Elsa/Getty Images; 14, © Dilip Vishwanat/Getty Images; 15, © Andrew Gombert/epa/Corbis; 16, © Jed Jacobsohn/Getty Images; 17, © Jonathan Daniel/Getty Images; 18, © Chuck Solomon/Sports Illustrated; 19, © Brad Mangin/ MLB Photos via Getty Images; 20, © Tannen Maury/epa/Corbis; 21, © REUTERS/ Peter Newcomb; 22T, © Jim McIsaac/Getty Images; 22C, © Jed Jacobsohn/Getty Images; 22B, © Brad Mangin/MLB Photos via Getty Images.

Publisher: Kenn Goin
Senior Editor: Lisa Wiseman
Creative Director: Spencer Brinker
Photo Researcher: Omni-Photo Communications, Inc.
Design: Stacey May

Library of Congress Cataloging-in-Publication Data

Sandler, Michael.
 David Eckstein and the St. Louis Cardinals : 2006 World Series / by Michael Sandler.
    p. cm. — (World Series superstars)
 Includes bibliographical references and index.
 ISBN-13: 978-1-59716-636-2 (library binding)
 ISBN-10: 1-59716-636-7 (library binding)
1. Eckstein, David, 1975—Juvenile literature. 2. Baseball players—United States— Biography—Juvenile literature. 3. St. Louis Cardinals (Baseball team) —Juvenile literature. 4. World Series (Baseball) (2006) —Juvenile literature. I. Title.

 GV865.E34S36 2008
 796.357092—dc22
 (B)
                              2007032667

For more information, write to Bearport Publishing Company, Inc., 101 Fifth Avenue, Suite 6R, New York, New York 10003. Printed in the United States of America.

10 9 8 7 6 5 4 3 2 1

★ Contents ★

No Chance

"It's impossible," said baseball fans. "There's no way the St. Louis Cardinals can win the 2006 World Series." The team had only won 83 games all season. Their **opponents**, the Detroit Tigers, were on fire. They had won 95 regular-season games. Everyone expected the Tigers to roll right over St. Louis.

Cardinals **shortstop** David Eckstein heard what people were saying. He knew his team was the **underdog**. It didn't bother him, though. David had been one all his life.

Fans support the Tigers

At just under 5'7" (1.70 m), David was the shortest player in the 2006 World Series.

Little Guy

David grew up in Sanford, Florida. The youngest in a family of five kids, he was always small for his age.

He loved baseball, but people said he was too little to play. Still, no one could keep him off the field.

David made up for his size with hard work. He learned how to **place** hits and **position** himself in the field. By high school, he was a talented **infielder**.

After high school, David played baseball for the University of Florida.

David slides into base.

David made the University of Florida team as a **walk-on**.

The Major Leagues

The Boston Red Sox **drafted** David in 1997. After a few years in the **minor leagues**, he joined the Anaheim Angels.

In 2001, he won a place on their **major league** team. He showed a great eye for the ball and rarely struck out.

Most of the time he batted **lead-off**. His job was to get on base and move into position to score. David was good at this job.

David won a World Series with the Angels in 2002.

In 2005, David joined the St. Louis Cardinals. He was voted to play in the **All-Star Game** that same season.

The St. Louis Cardinals

The Cardinals, nicknamed the Redbirds, were one of baseball's most successful teams. Hall-of-Famers such as Dizzy Dean, Lou Brock, Bob Gibson, and Ozzie Smith had all worn Cardinals uniforms.

The Redbirds had nine World Series wins, more than any other **National League** team. However, their last win had come in 1982. Getting the tenth **title** was proving hard.

Still, St. Louis began the 2006 season with high hopes. Sluggers like Albert Pujols and **Gold Glove** fielders like Jim Edmonds made the Redbirds feel confident.

Pitcher Bob Gibson won seven World Series games for the Cardinals.

Ozzie Smith (right) helped St. Louis beat the Milwaukee Brewers in the 1982 World Series.

Only the **American League**'s New York Yankees had more World Series wins than the Cardinals.

A Tough Season

The Cardinals got off to a roaring start in 2006. By early summer, David and his teammates were in first place.

Then things began to go wrong. Injuries struck many St. Louis players. David pulled a leg muscle and hurt his shoulder. The team began to lose one game after another.

St. Louis finished with an 83-78 record. They barely won more games than they lost. Somehow they still made it to the **playoffs**. Few people, however, thought they'd go very far.

Due to injuries, David missed almost 40 regular-season games.

First baseman Albert Pujols helped the Redbirds make it to the playoffs.

No team had ever won a World Series after losing so many regular-season games.

Playoff Surprise

In the playoffs, St. Louis came back to life. They rolled over the San Diego Padres and moved on to face the New York Mets.

The series was very close. After six games, the teams were tied with three wins each. Game 7 would decide the series.

In the ninth inning of Game 7, Cardinals catcher Yadier Molina smacked a home run. It broke the 1-1 tie. St. Louis held on to win. Amazingly, the Cardinals were headed to the World Series.

Pitcher Chris Carpenter helped the Cardinals win against the Padres.

Yadier Molina hit the game-winning home run in Game 7 against the Mets.

No one expected Yadier to hit the game-winning run. In the 2006 season, he was one of baseball's weakest hitters.

Here Comes Detroit

Despite their **upset** of the Mets, the Cardinals were still considered underdogs. Their World Series opponents, the Detroit Tigers, seemed like the stronger team.

In the playoffs, the Tigers quickly defeated the New York Yankees and the Oakland A's. This meant they had six days of rest while the Cardinals were busy playing the Mets.

Rested, talented, and powerful, the Tigers were sure to win. Everyone thought so, except the Cardinals themselves.

Detroit right fielder Magglio Ordoñez hit a three-run home run against Oakland.

Detroit celebrates their win over the Oakland A's.

Detroit lost just one playoff game on their way to the 2006 World Series.

Let the Games Begin

Detroit and St. Louis **split** the first two games. Although the series was tied, David wasn't happy. So far, he hadn't gotten a hit. He hadn't done his job of getting on base!

In Game 3, David finally snapped out of his **slump**. His two hits helped the Cardinals win, 5-0. Then, in Game 4, he really broke out. David slapped four more hits as St. Louis won, 5-4.

Anthony Reyes pitched the Redbirds to a Game 1 win.

David hit three doubles in Game 4.

After Game 4, Cardinals manager Tony LaRussa called David "the toughest guy I've ever seen in a uniform."

Taming the Tigers

David couldn't get a hit in the first two games of the World Series. Now, no one could get him out. Thanks to their shortest player, St. Louis was one win away from taking the series.

In Game 5, David came through again, knocking in the winning run. Finally, St. Louis had its tenth World Series title!

Many had doubted the Cardinals, but not David. "The funny thing about baseball is you never know," he said. "If you believe in yourself, you can do it."

The Cardinals celebrate their World Series win.

David was named Most Valuable Player (MVP) of the 2006 World Series. He is the shortest MVP in World Series history.

David, along with some other key players, helped the St. Louis Cardinals win the 2006 World Series.

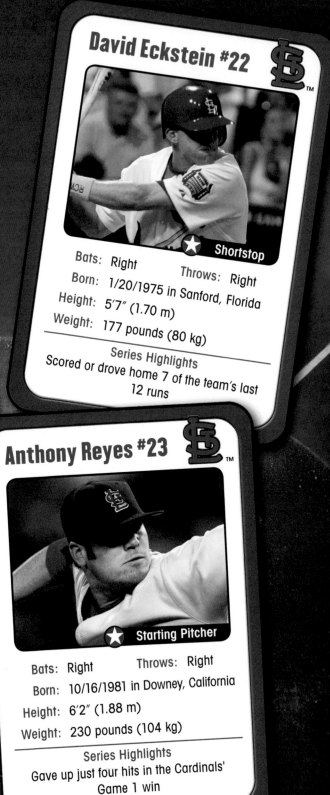

David Eckstein #22

Shortstop

Bats:	Right	Throws:	Right

Born: 1/20/1975 in Sanford, Florida

Height: 5′7″ (1.70 m)

Weight: 177 pounds (80 kg)

Series Highlights
Scored or drove home 7 of the team's last 12 runs

Scott Rolen #27

Third Base

Bats:	Right	Throws:	Right

Born: 4/4/1975 in Jasper, Indiana

Height: 6′4″ (1.93 m)

Weight: 240 pounds (109 kg)

Series Highlights
Hit .421 and scored five runs

Anthony Reyes #23

Starting Pitcher

Bats:	Right	Throws:	Right

Born: 10/16/1981 in Downey, California

Height: 6′2″ (1.88 m)

Weight: 230 pounds (104 kg)

Series Highlights
Gave up just four hits in the Cardinals' Game 1 win

★ Glossary ★

All-Star Game (AWL-STAR GAME) a yearly game between the National and American leagues; only the best players in each league get to play

American League (uh-MER-uh-kuhn LEEG) one of the two major professional baseball leagues in the United States

drafted (DRAFT-id) picked to play for a professional team

Gold Glove (GOHLD GLUHV) an award given to players for their outstanding fielding skills

infielder (IN-feel-dur) a player whose position is either first base, second base, third base, or shortstop

lead-off (LEED-awf) the player who bats first for a team at the start of a game or inning

major league (MAY-jur LEEG) the highest level of professional baseball in the United States, made up of the American League and the National League

minor leagues (MYE-nur LEEGZ) baseball teams run by the major-league teams that train young players

National League (NASH-uh-nuhl LEEG) one of the two major professional baseball leagues in the United States

opponents (uh-POH-nuhnts) teams or athletes who others play against in a sporting event

place (PLAYSS) to hit the ball in a certain spot on the field where it will not be caught

playoffs (PLAY-awfss) games held after the regular season to determine who will play in the World Series

position (puh-ZISH-uhn) to put oneself in the right spot on the field

shortstop (SHORT-*stop*) the player whose position is between second and third base

slump (SLUHMP) a period of time when a player is not playing well

split (SPLIT) to divide evenly

title (TYE-tuhl) the championship; in baseball, a World Series win

underdog (UHN-dur-*dawg*) an athlete or team who is not expected to win

upset (UHP-set) when the team expected to lose beats the team expected to win

walk-on (WAWK-on) a player who makes it on to a college team even though he wasn't offered a scholarship

Bibliography

Snyder, John. *Cardinals Journal*. Cincinnati, OH: Emmis Books (2006).

The New York Times

St. Louis Post-Dispatch

Sports Illustrated

Read More

Eckstein, David, with Greg Brown. *Have Heart*. Lake Mary, FL: Builder's Stone Publishing (2006).

O'Hearn, Mike. *The Story of the St. Louis Cardinals*. Mankato, MN: Creative Education (2007).

Savage, Jeff. *Albert Pujols*. Minneapolis, MN: Lerner (2007).

Learn More Online

To learn more about David Eckstein,
the St. Louis Cardinals, and the World Series, visit
www.bearportpublishing.com/WorldSeriesSuperstars

Index